HOW TO EARN MONEY FROM HOME EASILY

GET ONLINE JOBS FOR WOMEN AND MEN,
START AN ONLINE BUSINESS QUICKLY AND
EASILY FROM YOUR ROOM

Jessy M. Brown

Table of Contents

Introduction

You went to school and got your degree. You've spent years perfecting your skills and building a career. Now, you're a mother and your priorities are changing big time. However, thanks to the current economic climate, their need to earn money still exists.

Can you have it all? Can you be a full-time mother and still have a lucrative and rewarding career?

The answer is yes, if you learn to balance your life. One of the easiest ways to have it all and enjoy a sense of balance is to do things on your own and become a stay-at-home mom. With your professional experience, years of experience and determination, you can make it happen.

However, the shift from working in the field or in an office to working at home is a big step. Before immersing yourself in the prospectus, it's a very good idea to take stock of your chances of thriving at home. For some people, shining as a mother and excelling in the workplace requires a little separation. For others, work at home suits them perfectly.

Once you decide if working at home is right for you, there will be much more to do. The next step is to determine what your perspectives are and how to overcome some of the obstacles that will invariably stand in your way. Don't worry, you can jump over obstacles relatively easily if you really want to.

There are a variety of career opportunities for working mothers at home. If you do not wish to continue in your current field, you can transfer some of your skills to another area of specialization. There are even some amazing places to go for training or retraining, even from home, if you want something completely new.

If you're attracted to contract work, finding a job won't be a big problem. The world is changing. Thanks to this, many employers offer part-time, short-term and even long-term jobs over the Internet. These are perfect for home workers.

Once you start finding work, you'll probably have to put a few other things in place. Questions about home offices, benefits and other technical aspects are likely to arise. As you explore your opportunities, prepare your home office, and establish a life that doesn't involve being away from your child, this e-book is your guide.

Together we can make your dreams of working at home come true and still have time for your family reality!

You have to consider it...

When you look into your child's eyes, the idea of putting on a suit and going back to the office is likely to be a bit of an astonishment. Staying home and working at home can be an incredible experience for you and your little one. However, it can also be a budding nightmare. It all depends on how well you and your family can handle the transition. Some women and their families thrive best when work is kept on the job. Others shine in the home business environment. No matter what path you choose, as long as it works for you, it's perfect!

So *how can you determine if working at home is what you really like?*

First, you'll want to examine your financial situation. To successfully launch a career from the home office, it may be helpful to have a little room to breathe financially. Keep in mind, however, that by staying home, you'll also save a little money.

Beyond the dollar issues, there are questions you will have to ask yourself and also your spouse and family members. To make a real home-based business or move your career full-time home, you're going to need to have the right personality to do it. In addition, you may also need some serious family support.

Let's take a look at some of the things you'll want to consider to help you decide if working at home is for you.

➢ EXPLORING THE FINANCIAL SIDE OF THINGS

Working at home can be very lucrative for many mothers. However, it may require a little time to obtain a constant cash flow. With this in mind, there are a number of things you will want to examine before you decide to dive with both feet. If you find that the timing is not right, don't worry too much. You can still work in a home business on weekends or evenings and try to build it quickly so you can stay home full time in the blink of an eye.

The basics to consider with finances include:

Your monthly budget: Carefully review your monthly bills and the amount of contribution you make. Remove things from the budget that will no longer be in place, such as child care and transportation costs. Now, keep in mind that it may take a little time to build a business enough to cover bills and other expenses. If your contribution is essential to your family's bottom line, check your savings. Do you have enough to cover your contribution for at least three months? Six or twelve would be even better. Is this base covered? If not, consider transitioning to full-time work at home as you build a reserve fund to cover yourself. Taking a slow and steady path in the right direction is better than not taking the path at all! With a little time and dedication, you can make your dream come true.

Your Anticipated Additional Expenses: Starting a home business can cost you initial capital. In addition to making sure your family is covered financially during the transition, you will need cash to set up an office, purchase equipment, advertising, obtain licenses and perhaps insurance, etc. It is possible to get a small business loan for these things and also to help cover them during the initial months. Keep in mind, however, that this will start your business in the red. Sometimes it's better to save and open the books in black.

The "Red Zone" Estimate: Although you won't be able to plan exactly when your business will start making money a day, you can make a pretty solid estimate. Be realistic here and anticipate at least a period of three months for a good development. This will help you determine the amount of fill you need in your bank account to stay comfortable as you build your business.

The financial side of things can be a great consideration when you decide to stop working in an office and make the transition to your own business. Make sure the bases are covered. Some of the options that can help you include loans, grants, savings or even start working part-time with the business to build it. However, money is not your only concern.

Your personality

Working at home is perfect for some people, but not for others. Either way, it's perfectly fine as long as you know where you're standing. You can be an excellent mother and work away from home. For some people, working at home and trying to be full-time parents doesn't work for the benefit of everyone involved. It all comes down to personality.

So, *do you have what it takes to make a career at home?* Ask yourself these questions and answer honestly:

Am I self-disciplined? Work at home still works. Add an infant, toddler or toddler and the job becomes two into one safely. To run a business or even to bring your full-time job into a teleworking environment, you'll have to have discipline. If you're the type that tends to get lost when a boss isn't looking over your shoulder, leaving behind the world of day-to-day work might not be for you. There are ways to overcome this obstacle, but first a little self-discipline is needed.

Can I stand not having the interaction of an "adult"? Work at home means spending a lot of time with little people. Some mothers thrive on both jobs when they keep them apart. The truth is that working mothers at home often lack time to communicate with adults. For some, this is not a problem to overcome. Others, however, find that dealing with customers by phone or email is not enough for adult interaction.

Am I motivated enough to accomplish this? Work in an office tends to be motivating on its own. Even those who are late can thrive in an environment where deadlines are set by others, work is overlooked and a paycheck depends on performance. Working at home is really a different game. If you are motivated and have a history of being an entrepreneur, you are likely to do well.

Can I set the hours and keep them? Working at home presents the danger of preparing to work too much. It is often best to set "office hours" and stick to them. Of course, you'll want to take time off from time to time to visit a park, see a school play and so on. That's fine! The question is, can you follow a schedule without a boss on a regular basis?

Working at home sounds fun and rewarding. For many, it is. Others simply discover that they do not thrive in this environment. Be honest with yourself and you will choose the right path to follow.

➤ *THE FAMILY IN THE FIRST PLACE*

When you decide to work outside your home, you are not the only one who will be affected by the decision. Your husband, older children, and anyone else living in the house will also feel the effects. In most cases, having mom at home is a big deal. Families, however, will have to intervene and help. If they don't support your decision, your business could be dead in the water before it starts.

So, *what do you need from your family for your home business to succeed?* Make sure your family is willing to do that:

Help at home: It can be very tempting for family members to leave everything for you to do just because you are at home. While they may have helped with cooking, shopping, laundry, etc., when you worked outside the home, this could stop if you don't get proactive in setting the limits now. It's too easy for spouses and older children to think that just because mom is working at home, she's always more available to handle other tasks. Although you may be able to do more if you can do several tasks at once, you won't be able to do it every day.

Stay on board: Make sure you and your

partner fully discuss the idea of working at home before diving. If you don't have 100 percent support from your partner, you'll probably have to fight an uphill battle. Be sure to discuss the situation with an open mind. If there is resistance, share your business plan, budget, and other supporting materials. Chances are, your partner will like the idea of your child not being raised outside the home. Just make sure your partner is on board and he'll stay that way.

Helping in a pinch juggling life at home and in the office is difficult no matter what happens. If you're running your own business, there are times when you'll have to drop the proverbial ball on household chores, child care or something. With this in mind, it may be imperative for your business and your chances of success that you have contingency plans for emergencies. Is your spouse willing to take a day off to care for a sick child if you have a big sale you need to make? Will older children or grandparents pick up a younger child when you can't be there? Make sure you have a good support system and half of your battle will be won.

Working at home can sound glamorous and exciting. It's not always like this. It can present a series of obstacles that must be overcome to ensure success. Before diving into this adventure, you and your family should really explore whether this idea is right for you. If so, you can go at full speed to enjoy yourself while earning money and also to soak up time with your children.

The benefits of becoming a working mom can be staggering. If you desperately need more time with your children and want to be there for them, but still have financial obligations to your family, this may be the best solution. Simply take the time to examine the situation closely.

How to overcome obstacles?

No matter what type of business you expect to start or even if you intend to become a teleworker for your existing business, there will be obstacles you will have to face. From finances to your own fears of isolation, working at home all the time is not necessarily rainbows and sun every day. You'll have good days and bad days. You'll even face obstacles that stand in your way to even start. Fortunately, there are things you can do to deal with almost any obstacle that gets in your way.

✓ *FINANCIAL BLOCKS*

Perhaps the biggest obstacle that will stand in the way of starting a home-based business is the question of money. This may not apply if you are going to become a telecommuter for your existing company or another. However, if you start from scratch, it can be a big obstacle to overcome.

For the best basis to get started, take a close look at that budget as suggested earlier. If you fall short, these tips can help you get the money you need to make your dream come true:

Savings Plan: This may take longer than other options to overcome cash flow problems, but it can put you in a better financial position in the long run. Instead of borrowing money, this obstacle finder simply requires you to start building your business savings on your own. You can do this by staying at your regular job and saving money from your checks. You may also consider launching your business part-time at night to accumulate cash, contacts and income. The latter option keeps the money from your daily work and can increase it with the part-time company. In general, this is a fairly prudent way to overcome money problems.

Loans: Small business loans, mortgage refinances, second mortgages and other loan options may be available for you to start your business. This route can start your dream and give you cash in the bank to live for a while, too. The danger here is that you'll have to make the payments. Essentially, financing a business with loans involves starting with books in red. Still, if your business idea is good enough and your skills are high enough, it may be a good way to do it.

Subsidies: Sometimes it's possible to get grants to start a small business. This will depend a lot on what you plan to do. If you are eligible for grants, they are worth applying for. The fact is, grants can give you the money you need without having to pay anything. Government and foundation grants may be available. Consider the option, but plan a great application process. If you are successful in getting grants, make sure the money goes exactly where you said it would go as well. Otherwise, you can get to a lot of hot water!

Investors Family, friends or other acquaintances may want to enter your business on the ground floor. Although this is probably the least recommended option, it can feed your business dreams quite quickly. Count on having to repay these loans or offer a portion of your business to these "partners".

Money problems can always be overcome if you are determined to do so. Consider your options and go ahead with the option or options that work best for you.

✓ *FAMILY RESILIENCE*

Family resilience can also be a problem when you're considering becoming a working mom. If you don't have his full support, you could be in trouble.

Here are some tips for overcoming problems that may arise:

Highlight the benefits: Make sure your partner fully understands what your work at home can mean for your family. Although you will have duties to attend to, you will ultimately be more available to your family.

Talk to Savings Potential: Point out how much you are going to save on gas, lunches outside, fast food dinners and child care. These expenses can add up very quickly and can even compensate for any loss you would face by leaving your current job if that is your intention. Many moms find that they spend about the same as at work on these expenses that can be eliminated from a budget sheet if you work at home.

Highlight potential earnings: Make sure your family knows they've done the homework for your business idea. Show them profit protections, potential customers and so on. If you already have customers who have registered, this can be a quick change of heart for sure.

If your partner isn't sure you can do it, prove it. Start your business part-time and grow it carefully. Once it takes off, it will be possible to make the transition and not jeopardize the family's income. Keep in mind that your partner probably supports your decision 100 percent, but may fear "what if...". This is good. Just show your partner and yourself that you can do it.

Family endurance is generally very easy to overcome. If you've done your homework, you should be able to sell your plan pretty well.

However, if you are like most people, the hardest job to sell will be with yourself. You have to believe that you can do it to succeed in being a working mom at home. One of the biggest obstacles you'll face on this front is isolation.

✓ *FEARS OF ISOLATION*

Working at home can lead to a sense of isolation. Make no mistake; you'll have to be proactive on this front. Unless you are perfectly content to deal with people only by phone and email, you will want to make some provisions for a social life in advance. Keep in mind that some business ideas will have you out of the house more than others, but it is likely that you will want to make a plan to conquer and overcome fears of isolation.

So *how can you ensure that your needs for adult conversation, networking and interaction are met?* These things can be lifesavers for working mothers at home:

Join a group of mothers: This is a great way to get out of the house and spend some time with your little one away from your new "office". When you join a group of mothers, you can meet new people and nurture your need for conversation. At the same time, you will give your child much-needed interaction. Many mothers' groups offer a complete program of activities that you can choose from. Some even offer evening events to get you out of the house just with the girls.

If you're going to sell, work as a consultant or do anything that can get you out of the house, take advantage of the time at least once in a while. Although the plan is to work at home as much as possible, going out several times a week is not a bad thing. In fact, it may be good for you and your child. A small opportunity of landscapes and faces never hurts anyone!

Join networked workgroups: Take the time to join networked workgroups, your local chamber of commerce, or other business organizations. Do it and you can kill two birds with one stone. Not only will you enjoy the interaction of adults, but you will also be able to boost your business at the same time.

Go to the meetings: If you are going to work remotely or even as a consultant, be sure to attend meetings in person from time to time. This will get you out of here and give you time to recharge your batteries among other working adults.

Stay in touch with your friends: Trust the same support network you've had for years to keep it running when you work at home. Call your friends to go out at night with girls, have fun or watch movies on weekends. Just because you work at home now doesn't mean you can't get out of the house.

Plan Date Nights: Make time to date your spouse or partner. One night a week or even one night a month to work as a couple can be a much-needed change of pace. Plus, it can help keep your relationship fresh and strong.

Enjoy a hobby: Leave the house on your own looking for a hobby you've always wanted to do. Take a class, learn to play tennis, just do something you find interesting on a personal level. Volunteering can also be a great way to get out and do something nice. Even one hour a week driving meals to the elderly can have a big impact on your psyche. Keep in mind that doing nothing but work and taking care of your family will burn you quickly. You have to have something that's all yours, too. Even if it's an hour a month doing something you like, do it!

Don't worry about working at home making you an isolationist. You can overcome this obstacle quite easily.

More options

We've already established that you've been working on a career for some time. This gives you a small advantage when it comes to exploring your options. You have skills in place that could most likely translate into a telework career or a new business venture that is all yours. Now is the time to really explore your options and decide how you can make work at home work for you.

If you don't want to take your current skills into a new business venture, don't worry. There are options that require very little retraining time. Some business ideas are also quite intuitive, so don't think you have to be pigeonholed to do what you do now. Unless, of course, you want to!

Let's take a look at some of the options where you can open the door.

• *TELEWORKING FOR YOUR CURRENT EMPLOYER*

If you've been working for your current employer for a while and love the job, but want to stay home, telework may work for you. If your employer already uses teleworkers, you will have an advantage. If not, take the time to discuss it with your supervisor and superiors.

Telework is increasingly accepted in major workplaces. There are even a number of Fortune 500 companies that allow their employees to work from home all or part of the time. The benefits of taking your work home and staying with your current company can be extensive. These include

If you do at home what you already do in the office, the learning curve will be non-existent. This is a great way to have your cake and eat it, too.

Extension of Benefits: If you remain employed in your current company, you will not lose any of the benefits offered. This can be a big problem for some families, so don't discount the value.

Guaranteed Income: Your family won't lose a penny if you work remotely. In fact, you could end up earning more thanks to the savings on the costs of working at home that we've already discussed. This can be a great advantage for you and your family. It can also work well as a tool to convince your family that working at home is right for you.

Telework has its pros and cons. If you choose to stay with your current employer, you will be limited to a fixed salary. Most likely, your hours will also be monitored. This may take away some of the freedoms you expected to enjoy working at home. Carefully consider the ups and downs of this option before proceeding. Other options are available.

- **CONSULTING IN YOUR FIELD**

Okay, so maybe you don't want to work for your current employer anymore. Or, maybe you've discovered that your company simply doesn't allow teleworking for any reason. Don't take this as a barricade you can't get past. If you have developed your skills in a particular field, you may be able to transition to a consultant position.

If you decide to hire a consultant, you may be able to "work" for your company according to your terms and conditions. Please note, however, that you will lose your staff member status. This also means, however, that you can consult for other companies that can benefit from your knowledge, experience and skills.

Consultants are in great demand in a variety of fields. From legal and operational advisors to design, management and beyond, many companies turn to a set of external "eyes" on a regular basis. Many are also willing to pay a good price for professional consultants.

If you want to transition to a consultant position, consider the following to get your effort going:

Get close to your existing business: Depending on your skills, this may be the fastest way to enjoy a solid consulting contract. Your company may delight in the idea of taking you off the payroll and saving on benefits, but still have your skills available.

Join commercial organizations: To find other opportunities, be sure to join commercial organizations and stay current with the meetings, publications, and even online search ads these groups post. This can be a great way to find work in your field on a consulting basis.

Make sure you are on the government's list of offerings: Make sure you are on the list of city, county, state, and federal agency providers who could benefit from your skills. Government consulting contracts can overburden careers and offer stable incomes.

There are ways to stay in your existing field and use the skills you have perfected over time to earn money from home. However, if you want a complete change, there are ways to make it happen with little or no retraining. Of course, you can always retrain and jump in again if you want to enter a new field all together.

"Write" your goals

Writing for a living is one of the most stable and lucrative options for experienced homemakers. Freelance writers are in great demand in almost every field imaginable. As more companies take their business online, they need people to write their content, update their blogs, create special reports, etc. This option can allow you to work in your existing field, analyze, and also allow you to diversify into other interests.

If you want to put yourself in writing as your new business, you'll need to have some basic skills. Beyond being able to chain a sentence, you'll need to have a decent writing style, understand grammar, and be able to handle the pressures of deadlines.

Some of the options available to

freelance writers include:

    ✓ Blogging;
    ✓ Report writing;
    ✓ Public relations writing;
    ✓ Creation of Search Engine Optimization contents;
    ✓ Technical Writing.

Writing for a living can be an exciting and rewarding career option. For mothers who work at home and know how to write, the possibilities are almost limitless.

> ### DATA ENTRY AND OTHER SIMILAR

Typing may not be your thing, but that doesn't mean you can't put your keyboard skills to work. Data entry positions and other related jobs are always in high demand by the self-employed and remote workers. Having a vocational training can be a great boost to enter these fields, too.

Some of the related fields to consider beyond data entry include:

- ✓ Medical billing;
- ✓ Medical transcription;
- ✓ Transcription;
- ✓ Work as an online personal assistant;
- ✓ Billing agent.

-

➢ **SALES**

If your skills are in the sales area, you will find a world of possibilities open to you. The reality is that selling is one of the easiest ways to get into a business, but it can be one of the hardest to achieve. Still, if you're good at it, the sky will be the limit.

If sales seem good to you, related options include:

Working as a great representative, established companies that sell household goods, cosmetics and other similar products recruit salespeople all the time. In these cases, the vendors are independent contractors who set their own schedules, work in their own territories, etc. This can be a great way to enjoy "owning" a business without having to reinvent the wheel.

Franchise Possibilities: This is another great way to go if you want to own your own business and reap all the rewards. Franchising can give your business instant recognition and the support you need to get off to a good start.

Other Possibilities: It is possible to turn a hobby into a business, create a product to produce and sell, launch a website and so on. These options may depend on the skills you already have or allow you to develop new ones to follow a completely different path. Don't leave any stone unturned on this front if you want to do something completely different.

The possibilities of working at home are limited only by imagination. Whether you want to stay in your existing field or diversify into a whole new direction, there are ways to make your dreams of working at home come true. Just take the time to really explore your options, do your homework and see which path works best for you and your family. If you need retraining or new skills, relax. You can start training a little easier than you think.

Your learning

You've made a decision, explored your options, and discovered that some kind of training will be necessary for your dreams to come true. Don't worry too much. There are many options available to you to make sure you get the training you need. In many cases, you can continue to work at your day job and study online or go to school at night. In some cases, it may even be possible to launch your new career at home while receiving additional training to strengthen your business.

So *what are your options for getting the training you need?* There are three main options to consider: college, technical schools, or certification programs.

- *GO BACK TO COLLEGE*

If you want to make a dramatic change in the fields, college may be the best option for you. Thanks to online degree programs, however, this doesn't have to be as daunting as it sounds. It is possible to work during the day and attend classes at night.

To make it easier to get back to school, consider these tips:

There are tons of scholarship programs and grants for women. Explore each option and leave no stone unturned. Many of these grants and scholarships are now also available for online undergraduate courses. Also pay close attention to scholarships for working mothers. There are organizations that will pay the entire bill for moms looking for new careers.

If you already have a degree, you may only need a few courses to get the training you need. Keep that in mind. If you need a full programme of study, concentrate on the future to move forward.

Of course you want to be in business

right now! If this isn't possible, don't rush too fast. Working, going to school and taking care of a family can be a lot of work. Try to take only what is reasonable and work firmly toward the ultimate goal.

Going back to college and getting a new degree can be a great way to retrain for a new career. It may take a little longer than other options, but it's a good way to start over.

- ### *TECHNICAL SCHOOLS*

Technical schools can provide the necessary training for a variety of careers. From designing and selling websites to repairing computers and beyond, this option can be excellent for several reasons. These include

Costs: Technical schools, especially if they are state or county schools, tend to be much more affordable than college.

Programming: Technical schools tend to have very flexible schedules. In many cases, courses of study can be quite short, but still provide the skills needed to start a new career.

Targeted Learning: Technical programs do not involve many "extra" courses that standard university degrees tend to require. This may allow you to go straight to the point rather than having to turn the wheels on Basket Weaving 101.

• *CERTIFICATION PROGRAMS*

Short-term certification programs may be the perfect solution for certain professional fields. Medical transcription, billing and even web design, for example, can often be learned during "intensive course" certification programs. This is an excellent way to do it for a number of reasons, among them:

Time Involved: Certification programs are usually very short in duration, but provide the training necessary to succeed in certain professional fields. When certifications are combined with an existing degree, a general curriculum can be very attractive.

Costs Involved: Although the prices of certification programs will vary, of course, they are generally much more affordable than full degree programs.

Targeted Learning: Like technical schools, certification programs also provide a very specific learning course. This is excellent for those who don't want to spend a lot of time in courses that have nothing to do with the ultimate goal of their career.

If your business of choice will require some kind of retraining to enjoy success, don't panic. There are options available to you that can accelerate the learning effort. It is even possible to keep costs down in many cases thanks to grants and scholarships. Don't let training get in the way of your dreams.

The right jobs

You have selected your field, designed your plans and are ready to go. The question now is how to start making money. Unless you're working remotely for an existing employer, you're going to need a game plan to get some business. At first, getting the right jobs will probably take up a lot of your work. However, there are methods that can help you. What works best will depend on your exact pursuit.

- ## *ADVERTISING PAYS*

Whether you intend to sell a product or a service, advertising will be vital to your business. Your real field can, however, impact the best places to put your advertising dollars. To start getting customers, consider these potential advertising vehicles:

Local Sources: Community newspapers, television stations and radio stations can be a good starting point if you don't want to expand your business beyond your region. Depending on the type of race you intend to pursue in your country, these vehicles can provide an incredible boost to a business.

Commercial publications: If you intend to consult, commercial publications can provide the key to opening the door to success. Advertising in these publications will put your company name in the spotlight with people from fields that might need your help.

Websites make the difference: No matter in which field you enter, it can be very useful to advertise your company online. If you are selling, you can sell directly online. If you provide a service, you can get business by using a Web site to promote it. Companies that have Web sites used to be a rarity. Today, this is considered a hallmark of a professional company. Even consultants have their own sites and sometimes blogs to explain what they do, how they do it and why they should do the work.

Creative advertising: If you plan to sell a product or provide a service that the general population can use, such as accounting, bookkeeping, etc., creative advertising can help you get started. Billboards, bank ads, brochures and other similar options can help you get your business to its destination.

- ***EMPLOYMENT SERVICES CAN HELP***

Going to consulting or even offering skills as a freelance may be a good way to do it. In order to get jobs in this field, it can sometimes be useful to work directly with employment agencies. Since employers are usually the ones who pay for these services, you have nothing to lose by following this route and everything to gain.

Some of the benefits of working with employment services include:

Have access to your contacts: Established employment agencies tend to have a long list of clients. This means they can potentially make you walk through the door with contracts you haven't even dreamed of getting.

The Defending Factor: Employment services do not earn money unless they find the right professionals for the job. To this end, they work hard to match freelancers, consultants and private contractors directly with the companies that can use their services. It never hurts to have the advocates on your side when you're trying to start an adventure at home!

The specialty factor: There are employment agencies that specialize in dealing with contractors and consultants. There are even those who work exclusively in a particular field. Connecting with the right agency can really open doors and serve as an incredible springboard for your home business.

- ### *WEBSITES CAN BE AN EXCELLENT CHOICE*

If your plan is to work more or less in the online arena, being online not only with your own site, but also through employment websites can really pay off. A large number of employment-related websites have emerged to connect the self-employed and small business owners with potential contract employers. The advantages of using services of this type include:

Low costs: The best online job search services charge a membership fee, but overall, prices tend to be low. For a few dollars a quarter, you may find yourself with more jobs than you can handle.

Bidding processes: Just for this reason, going through online employment services can be very useful. If you intend to work as a contractor or consultant, going through the online bidding processes can help you see where you might need to make improvements. If, for example, you're not being aggressive enough, you'll learn quickly. In addition, some RFx environments are open. This means that you will be able to see what your competition is charging. This can help you stay competitive and get jobs in the future.

Exposure: Online job sites tend to attract a wide variety of potential employers. In many cases, employers can come from all over the world. The exposure you and your business can gain by using these sites is incredible.

Training: In addition to learning to manage the competition, the whole process of going online to get business can serve as a great training for other companies. Once you master the preparation of bid packages, for example, you may be better prepared to go through a government bidding process.

• *THE FRANCHISES*

Franchisees tend to have a head start. If you have opted for this route, you will benefit from some things right away when it comes to landing business to start. These things include:

Training: Most large franchises and even some of the smaller ones offer training not only in the business model, but also in advertising and marketing.

Instant Recognition: Franchises have the advantage of having a recognized name. This in itself can bring business immediately. If you choose a franchise that is less well known, make sure you have a good business model and a quality product or service. It is good to enter the ground floor as the reconnaissance is being built. Just make sure the company is really one you can back up. If you're not convinced of a company, chances are no one else is.

Group advertising: Many franchises conduct national advertising campaigns. They do this by using some of the franchise fees that come in. In some cases, franchisees in a local area may also choose to do "group shopping" to take advantage of more advertising. Each franchisee in a region, for example, will kick in X amount of dollars for a big campaign. This increases exposure without costing the business owner too much money.

• *WORK NETWORK*

No matter what field you have decided to work in, if you intend to own your own work at home, networking will be important. In short, this is another form of advertising. This, however, does not have to cost too much and can be amortized with a ton of rewards.

There are a number of options on the front of the networks. The best option or options for you will depend on the type of business you plan to get into. Some of your networking options include:

Chambers of Commerce: No matter what field you intend to enter, this can be an excellent option to reach your local market. When you join a camera, not only will you make your business known, but you'll also benefit from the opportunity to get away from the 'home office'. In addition, many cameras offer valuable business training sessions at a very low cost to members.

Online networks: There are online groups that help business owners operating on the web get to know each other. This is a great way to reach out to other entrepreneurs. If you intend to work as a contractor or consultant, these groups can also yield results with some serious business.

Networking Groups: Like local chambers of commerce, these groups can be very beneficial in making your name known in your community. Networking groups also provide a rather beneficial social and educational function. It never hurts to have other people in your situation to talk to and learn from.

Sponsorships: This is a different way to get your company's name to the local community, but it may be worth it. Sponsor a local event, a sports team, a class. Make your name known to people who will recognize you for your loyalty to the community and pay you with their support.

Getting the right jobs may require a concerted effort. You will need to know where to look, how to spread the word about yourself and how to establish a proper network. Don't worry if you've never done this before. It will come to you in time. Advertising is the easy part, but it'll cost money. Networking can be a bit difficult for the shy, but this can be as important as any type of paid ad you can find.

How to set up a home office?

You've made a decision and you plan to work at home. Good for you! Even if you have your chosen field, the money in place and a business plan all ready to go, there is still more work to be done. Perhaps one of the biggest and most important steps has not yet been taken. To work at home and be successful, you need a place to call your own.

Yes, of course, you want to be with your family and in the middle of all this. Still, if you don't have an office to call yours when you need it, you may be very sorry. The fact is that making phone calls to customers with a small child screaming in the background can be embarrassing. Writing reports about the deadline while your family watches television can be a distraction. To overcome and conquer these problems, you will need a home office. Plus, having one will give you a built-in tax deduction!

For a home office to really work for you, it's worth exploring what you really need. It is also a good idea to remember why it is important to have your own space.

➢ *WHAT YOU NEED*

A home office doesn't need to be elaborate to be effective. The amount or amount of space required will depend on your own personal tastes and the space you have available. In general, as long as there are utility connections - telephone, cable, etc. - and a door, you must be ready. Even useful problems can be solved with wireless networks and extension cables.

Beyond space, you probably need these things to set up a home office properly:

A desk: Elaborate is not important here. You can go as basic as using a piece of wood placed on top of two file cabinets. As long as you have a workspace for your important papers and files and are well on this front.

Computer and other equipment: Almost any field you enter will require a computer these days. If you intend to telework for your current employer, this is probably a necessity. Even if you want to start a new career, having a computer to work on can be very wise. Invest in a good machine and make sure you have a backup as well. Nothing can set aside a business faster than computer problems! It might also be a good idea to consider online hard drive backup services to make sure your bases are covered in case of an accident. Beyond the basic configuration of a computer, you will need to consider such things as a phone, a copier and a fax. If your field requires special equipment, you will also need to plan for it.

One door: Once again, you don't have to work at the central office all the time. If you want to be in the kitchen with a laptop while you prepare dinner, you're the boss! However, having a door to close when necessary may be imperative for concentration. It can also help remind you that you are "on the clock". In addition, having a door can also remind family members that you are "on the clock. Remember, your family may have a long enough adjustment period for you to work at home. The private space can serve as a great reminder that the fact that mom is home doesn't mean she can handle every single problem that arises.

➤ *WHY DO YOU NEED A HOME OFFICE?*

Even if your home is small and finding a space to sculpt it is a challenge, make it happen. Whether you're guarding a garage corner, using a closet or claiming an extra room, just claim a space!

The reasons why this is so important include:

✓ Privacy;
✓ Professionalism;
✓ Tax deduction, which can be very important;
✓ Your sanity!

A home office can be a bit complicated to create, but it may be worth giving you the space you need to work. No matter what your work at home is, privacy will be appreciated. You can count on it!

> ## *TIPS FOR SUCCESS*

While the road to success can vary greatly depending on the business you plan to follow, there are some general tips that can help you no matter what. Some of the best tips for mothers include:

Be patient: Working at home can be very rewarding. It can also be terribly frustrating. When your 8-year-old tells you the same story for the fifth time while you're on a deadline, your patience may run out. Take a deep breath, count to 10 and explain that you'd love to hear it in a while.

Believe in yourself: Since you are not a stranger in the world of work thanks to your original career, you should have an advantage in this case. Still, it can be very discouraging to have your own business and not have a "company" to turn to. Believe in yourself, take stock of your abilities and move forward at full speed. If you were able to enjoy a successful career working for someone else, there's no reason you can't do it all for yourself!

Set work hours: This can't be stressful enough. You have to establish a routine during most days to be able to work at home. If you'd rather spend the whole day with your kids, do it. Just make sure you "punch in" when you go to bed. You have to stick with her to make an adventure at home.

Promote yourself: Take the time to

spread the word about your business. If you don't do it, no one else will. Your ultimate success will lie not only in your skills, but also in how well you do it to attract customers and contracts.

Be persistent: Launching any type of business requires time and dedication. If you're working at home, you'll still face the same obstacles that any company faces. You'll have to be diligent and persistent to overcome them.

Keep your contacts open: You are leaving a career in a company to stay at home with your family and start your own business. Make sure you keep the contacts you've made over the years open. They can be valuable sources of business for you in the future. This won't matter if you stay in your field or if you plan to follow a slightly different path. The reality is that your current reputation can help you a lot no matter what field you enter. Let your old contacts know what you're doing and keep you and your company at the forefront of their minds.

Be realistic: Don't expect to build a Fortune 500 company from your garage in 10 days or less. Although this is a fantastic goal, it is not prudent to expect such success from the outset. You may become discouraged and harm your chances of enjoying your goal. Just make sure your expectations are realistic.

Learn to multitask: You have decided to stay home for one reason - your family. Make sure you save them time. As you work in your business, this may mean you need to do several tasks at once. Learn how to prepare dinner while you're on the phone. Make calls while sitting in line at your child's school car. Prepare mass mailings while watching TV with the family at night.

Don't forget yourself: It can be very tempting to put everything you have into your family and your business. While this may sound like a great idea, it could burn you quickly. Make sure you buy yourself some time. This will help you relax, relax and recharge. Even 20 minutes a day reading a series of favorite books, meditating or jogging can give you the time you need to be yourself. Overlook this and your family, your business and all of you will probably suffer.

The benefits...

Unless you've decided to telework for your current employer, this is likely to be a question that will keep you awake at night. Even when you have your homework done and your business ready to start, the issue of profits can burn unanswered.

So how can you fill the gaps that will arise when you leave full-time employment for a position at your creation's home?

Fortunately, you have some options. Most working mothers can cover their bases in terms of health insurance, retirement and even savings. Don't let this particular obstacle act as a stumbling block.

> ## ➢ MEET MEDICAL NEEDS

Medical, dental, and vision coverage are generally among the biggest concerns for professional women who plan to move to a home-based business. Options are available. What works best for you will depend on your family's unique situation. Some of the options you may want to explore include:

Putting the family on your "Meaningful Couple" insurance: If your partner has insurance through your workplace, your settlement is quite easy. You and the children can be added to your policy. Most companies will allow mid-year changes like this if a big event has occurred in a family. In the worst case, you will have to wait until open enrollment.

Private policy options: It is possible to purchase private insurance to cover you and your family. However, keep in mind that many private purchase policies do not cover pre-existing conditions. Some medical conditions will, in fact, make it impossible to purchase private policies for individuals.

Group Options: This is a solution for those with pre-existing conditions. It is possible to put a home-based business into a group pool. The end result will be a policy much like that offered by a regular employer. This means that someone with a medical condition cannot be denied coverage. The disadvantage is the fact that costs can be quite high. However, the option may be a good solution for those who need it.

Covering your medical needs may not be as difficult or as expensive as you think. Explore all the options closely and choose the one that best suits your family.

➤ *RETIREMENT...*

Health insurance is the first and biggest concern women professionals have when they decide to make the transition to work at home. It's not the last one, though. Making sure retirement benefits or savings are in place can be just as important.

Please note that you will be your own boss in most of the scenarios we have discussed. This means that if you don't save for retirement, no one else is likely to do it on your behalf.

So *how can you make sure you have a savings nest for your Golden Years?* These options are available to you:

Individual Retirement Accounts: Individual accounts can be very beneficial in saving for the future. Not only do they tend to offer good interest rate gains, but they can also offset their gains when it's tax time. However, due to contribution limitations, you may want to have more than this card in your sleeve.

401ks: This retirement savings vehicle can put another vehicle into your retirement savings plan. You'll need to consult with a retirement investment company about how to start one. However, if you incorporate your business, this option must be open to you.

Stocks and Bonds: These may turn out to be a little high risk, but they can be rewarded with big rewards. Step carefully here, though, and don't put all your eggs in one basket.

Other options: There are many other investment vehicles that can help you replace a company-backed retirement account. Consider investing in gold, real estate and other similar tangible investments. If your business is one that could eventually be sold, this could also count as a retirement investment.

Just because your former employer doesn't fund a retirement policy doesn't mean you can't save for your future. With a good plan and a little discipline, you can make sure you have a reservation to make your Golden Years more comfortable.

➢ *OTHER SAVINGS*

Retirement won't or shouldn't be the only savings you consider when launching a new home-based business. You will probably also want a rainy day fund to be set up. This can be used to cover your business in periods of slow time. You may also want it for general savings for vacations, home improvements and emergencies.

Options to make your money work better with respect to overall savings include:

Money Market Accounts: This type of savings vehicle won't earn you a small fortune, but you can ensure that your money saved will earn something. Most banks offer these services and offer interest so you can let your money work for you.

U.S. Savings Short-Term Bonds: Bonds and other short-term businesses can be a good way to earn a little more from your savings.

Easy to Liquidate Investments: Some investments such as gold, collectible coins or stamps may also work well for rainy day savings. These can also be a good way to earn some money without taking a big risk in the process. It is not prudent to use them as the only form of savings, but they can be included in an overall plan.

Replacing benefits is not as difficult as it might seem. Vehicles are available for most stay at home moms to make base coverage possible.

How to successfully manage home and work

If you're used to working in an office and having a clear demarcation between work and family life, juggling can be a big challenge. The reality is that if you are making the conscious decision to be a home-working mom - even if you work remotely - you will be blurring the lines that create boundaries. To balance everything, you'll need a plan.

These tips can help:

Learn to Prioritize: Since you'll be the one at home, you'll probably have a lot more on your plate. You will feel compelled not only to take care of your child and your business, but also of your home. You can't do everything. Learning to prioritize what should be done and what you can expect will be essential. In the same way, we will also learn to delegate some duties to other family members when possible.

Learn to let go of a few things: If you have a sick child and a big contract at stake, your priorities are clear. Those two things will demand your attention. If your clothes pile up and your dishes don't wash, let them go. They'll wait till tomorrow. Your son and your client won't!

Learn how to ask for help: You're unbelievable, but you're only human. He'll need help sometimes. Don't be afraid to ask.

Have a backup plan: There will be a few days when you won't be able to keep up with your child and his work as well. Make sure you have a backup plan in place. Get a relative to care for the child or even to care for the child in a local day care center. It's okay not to always be the caregiver. In fact, sometimes children do better with socialization if they are allowed to be in groups from time to time.

Make the most of downtime: Take advantage of any downtime you have to address projects that need to be completed. While your baby sleeps, for example, make your calls. As your child eats breakfast, start preparing dinner in a slow cooker. Remember to buy yourself some time too.

Moving from a woman who works in an office to a mom who works at home can be a big transition. Be nice to yourself and learn to keep things in perspective. You can juggle a lot of balls at once. However, you can't do all the time alone.

Conclusion

Working at home isn't for everyone. Be sure to really explore the options and consider your motivations. If you know that you live and breathe working in an office with many people around you, you may not be happy at home. Although it sounds good to be able to spend time with your child, if you really want to be in an office with people, you can make everyone feel miserable if you do it differently. If your personality doesn't fit the profile of work at home, don't panic. You can have a career away from home and still be an excellent mother. Recognizing that you need something different may be good for your child.

Now, if you have decided that moving is really good for you, your chances of enjoying success should increase. To really take a serious step in any career at home, you'll need to have a plan in place. This will have to include start-up funding, a business plan and even some prospects for advertising, marketing and a customer base. Do your homework and go ahead with caution. In no time, your business should be up and running.

Remember that while working at home, your playing field has changed dramatically. You will have to be able to juggle, exercise patience and maintain a sense of humour about yourself. The job will be important, but so will your other job: being a mom.

Set your goals and try to meet them. However, exercise some flexibility. There will be days when you can't get into the "office" until midnight and others when everything flows smoothly from morning routine to bedtime. The beauty of being a mom who works at home is that you must have the ability to adapt to the needs of the day. This particular benefit may be worth every bit of effort needed to launch a home business.

Becoming a working mom at home is very important for a career woman. Stand firm and be patient. If you do this, you can make your dreams come true.

Just remember that everything will not happen overnight and that it will take time before you see a change in your life for the better.

Now yes, I wish you the best in your results, and remember, everything is practical; theory without action is of no use to you.

A big hug, your friend, Jessy!

By the way, when you achieve your results little by little, I highly recommend you, if you want to learn much more about methods of making money, the book of a great author from whom I learn a lot, on "SECRET STRATEGIES TO MAKE A LOT OF MONEY IN THE MULTINIVEL BUSINESS", is a book that I am sure will help you a lot on your way to "financial freedom".

Without further ado, you can find it in the Amazon search engine, such as: "Secret strategies to earn a lot of money in the multi-level business" or looking for its name, such as: "Gaston Echevarria"... Once again I wish you success in your results!